SIX / SEVEN

WHAT GOD SAYS

REV. MIKE EASTER

APOCRYPHILE
PRESS

Apocryphile Press
PO Box 255
Hannacroix, NY 12087
www.apocryphilepress.com

Copyright © 2025 by Rev. Mike Easter
Printed in the United States of America
ISBN 978-1-965646-59-5 | paper
ISBN 978-1-965646-60-1 | ePub

Please join our mailing list at www.apocryphilepress.com/free. We'll keep you up-to-date on all our new releases, and we'll also send you a FREE BOOK. Visit us today!

CONTENTS

PART TWO
NEW TESTAMENT

INTRODUCTION

Six Seven… Six Seven… Six… Seven…

You hear it, don't you? You don't even need an annoying child in your class—your brain supplies one automatically. The sing-song voice, the rhythm, the unstoppable repetition. It's like seeing a picture of a Thanksgiving dinner on the cover of a grocery-store magazine. You don't have the dinner… but somehow you can *smell* it.

Six-Seven. Six-Seven. Six-Seven.

Always paired with that little hand gesture that means absolutely nothing.

Or does it?

People say this cloying bit of slang was birthed by a Mr. Skrilla and his mystical Doot-Doot song and accompanying video. (Because what the church really needed, after 2,000 years of theology, was *that*.) Forget the great works of Shakespeare or hymns like *A Mighty Fortress Is Our God*—apparently all we needed to get young Christians to pay attention was…

Doot. Doot.

But what if Mr. Skrilla is not merely a rapper… but a vessel? What if this humble troubadour of the internet is an unwitting instrument of the Most High? What if his chant—"Six Seven, Six Seven"—is actually a divine push notification nudging us back to Scripture?

Let us go back. Many years ago, early Christians gathered in a committee meeting that makes every church committee since look like a casual chat in a parking lot. They had to decide which poems, songs, laws, stories, and histories merited being placed between two covers.

They organized these treasures into books—Genesis, Exodus,

Constipations—each with chapters, and each chapter with numbered verses. And they called this book...

The Bible.

Fun Fact: This communion of church elders spent the first *two years* of their meeting arguing about the cover. Real leather? Faux laminent? Plain paper? That tissue-thin stuff we give preschoolers so they can feel holy? Two years. Just on the cover. And you thought your church committee was slow.

There was also a brief, regrettable period in the '70s and '80s (known historically as "the time of silliness") when publishers thought they could rename the Bible. They trotted out titles like *The Way* and *The Message,* but fortunately the better angels intervened before someone suggested *Extreme Scriptures* or *Holy Book: Now With More Action!*

Now, the Doot-Doot method of calling out the numbers six and seven may actually be a coded invitation—an invitation to look up these chapters and verses and discover what the Bible might be whispering (or shouting) into our current age of trials, tribulations.

Of course, because these verses are being lifted wildly out of context, it is up to each reader to interpret what the Holy of Holies desires us to know. Naturally, when left properly in context, the Bible needs no interpretation whatsoever and is perfectly clear to literally everyone all the time.

In the following pages, we present the seventh verse of the sixth chapter of each of the Bible's 80-something books for your study and reflection. For those books that don't have six chapters, we've taken the sixth and seventh verses of the first chapter. The illustrations—while beautiful—are not historically biblical, as the original Bible had no pictures due to early Christians tragically lacking crayons. These images are simply here to help guide the minds of those who need a little visual jump-start before thinking holy thoughts.

The Rev. Mike Easter

PART ONE
OLD TESTAMENT

GENESIS 6:7

"And the LORD said, I will destroy man whom I have created from the face of the earth; both man, and beast, and the creeping thing, and the fowls of the air; for it repenteth me that I have made them."

"**A**nd I will take you to me for a people, and I will be to you a God: and ye shall know that I am the LORD your God, which bringeth you out from under the burdens of the Egyptians."

LEVITICUS 6:7

"**A**nd the priest shall make an atonement for him before the LORD: and it shall be forgiven him for any thing of all that he hath done in trespassing therein."

NUMBERS 6:7

"**H**e shall not make himself unclean for his father, or for his mother, for his brother, or for his sister, when they die: because the consecration of his God is upon his head."

DEUTERONOMY 6:7

"And thou shalt teach them diligently unto thy children, and shalt talk of them when thou sittest in thine house, and when thou walkest by the way, and when thou liest down, and when thou risest up."

JOSHUA 6:7

"And he said unto the people, Pass on, and compass the city, and let him that is armed pass on before the ark of the LORD."

JUDGES 6:7

"And it came to pass, when the children of Israel cried unto the LORD because of the Midianites..."

RUTH 1:6–7

"Then she arose with her daughters in law, that she might return from the country of Moab: for she had heard in the country of Moab how that the LORD had visited his people in giving them bread. Wherefore she went forth out of the place where she was, and her two daughters in law with her; and they went on the way to return unto the land of Judah."

1 SAMUEL 6:7

" **N**ow therefore make a new cart, and take two milch kine, on which there hath come no yoke, and tie the kine to the cart, and bring their calves home from them…"

2 SAMUEL 6:7

"And the anger of the LORD was kindled against Uzzah; and God smote him there for his error; and there he died by the ark of God."

1 KINGS 6:7

"And the house, when it was in building, was built of stone made ready before it was brought thither: so that there was neither hammer nor axe nor any tool of iron heard in the house, while it was in building."

BARBANT

2 KINGS 6:7

"Therefore said he, Take it up to thee. And he put out his hand, and took it."

1 CHRONICLES 6:7

"**M**eraioth begat Amariah, and Amariah begat Ahitub..."

2 CHRONICLES 6:7

"Now it was in the heart of David my father to build an house for the name of the LORD God of Israel."

EZRA 6:7

"Let the work of this house of God alone; let the governor of the Jews and the elders of the Jews build this house of God in his place."

NEHEMIAH 6:7

" **A**nd thou hast also appointed prophets to preach of thee at Jerusalem, saying, There is a king in Judah: and now shall it be reported to the king according to these words. Come now therefore, and let us take counsel together."

ESTHER 6:7

"And Haman answered the king, For the man whom the king delighteth to honour..."

JOB 6:7

"The things that my soul refused to touch are as my sorrowful meat."

PSALM 6:7

"**M**ine eye is consumed because of grief; it waxeth old because of all mine enemies."

PROVERBS 6:7

"**W**hich having no guide, overseer, or ruler…"

ECCLESIASTES 6:7

"All the labour of man is for his mouth, and yet the appetite is not filled."

SONG OF SOLOMON 6:7

"As a piece of a pomegranate are thy temples within thy locks."

ISAIAH 6:7

"And he laid it upon my mouth, and said, Lo, this hath touched thy lips; and thine iniquity is taken away, and thy sin purged."

JEREMIAH 6:7

" **A**s a fountain casteth out her waters, so she casteth out her wickedness: violence and spoil is heard in her; before me continually is grief and wounds."

LAMENTATIONS 1:6–7

"And from the daughter of Zion all her beauty is departed: her princes are become like harts that find no pasture, and they are gone without strength before the pursuer. Jerusalem remembered in the days of her affliction and of her miseries all her pleasant things that she had in the days of old, when her people fell into the hand of the enemy, and none did help her: the adversaries saw her, and did mock at her sabbaths."

EZEKIEL 6:7

" **A**nd the slain shall fall in the midst of you, and ye shall know that I am the LORD."

DANIEL 6:7

"*All the presidents of the kingdom, the governors, and the princes, the counsellors, and the captains, have consulted together to establish a royal statute, ... that whosoever shall ask a petition of any God or man for thirty days, save of thee, O king, he shall be cast into the den of lions.*"

HOSEA 6:7

"**B**ut they like men have transgressed the covenant: there have they dealt treacherously against me."

JOEL 1:6–7

"For a nation is come up upon my land, strong, and without number, whose teeth are the teeth of a lion, and he hath the cheek teeth of a great lion. He hath laid my vine waste, and barked my fig tree: he hath made it clean bare, and cast it away; the branches thereof are made white."

AMOS 6:7

"Therefore now shall they go captive with the first that go captive, and the banquet of them that stretched themselves shall be removed."

OBADIAH 1:6-7

"How are the things of Esau searched out! how are his hidden things sought up! All the men of thy confederacy have brought thee even to the border: the men that were at peace with thee have deceived thee, and prevailed against thee; they that eat thy bread have laid a wound under thee: there is none understanding in him."

JONAH 1:6-7

"So the shipmaster came to him, and said unto him, What meanest thou, O sleeper? arise, call upon thy God, if so be that God will think upon us, that we perish not. And they said every one to his fellow, Come, and let us cast lots, that we may know for whose cause this evil is upon us. So they cast lots, and the lot fell upon Jonah."

MICAH 6:7

"Will the LORD be pleased with thousands of rams, or with ten thousands of rivers of oil? …"

NAHUM 1:6–7

"Who can stand before his indignation? and who can abide in the fierceness of his anger? his fury is poured out like fire, and the rocks are thrown down by him. The LORD is good, a strong hold in the day of trouble; and he knoweth them that trust in him."

HABAKKUK 1:6–7

"For, lo, I raise up the Chaldeans, that bitter and hasty nation, which shall march through the breadth of the land, to possess the dwellingplaces that are not theirs. They are terrible and dreadful: their judgment and their dignity shall proceed of themselves."

ZEPHANIAH 1:6–7

" **A**nd them that are turned back from the LORD; and those that have not sought the LORD, nor enquired for him. Hold thy peace at the presence of the Lord GOD: for the day of the LORD is at hand: for the LORD hath prepared a sacrifice, he hath bid his guests."

HAGGAI 1:6–7

"Ye have sown much, and bring in little; ye eat, but ye have not enough; ye drink, but ye are not filled with drink; ye clothe you, but there is none warm; and he that earneth wages earneth wages to put it into a bag with holes. Thus saith the LORD of hosts; Consider your ways."

ZECHARIAH 6:7

"And the bay went forth, and sought to go that they might walk to and fro through the earth..."

MALACHI 1:6–7

"A son honoureth his father, and a servant his master: if then I be a father, where is mine honour? and if I be a master, where is my fear? saith the LORD of hosts unto you, O priests, that despise my name. And ye say, Wherein have we despised thy name? Ye offer polluted bread upon mine altar; and ye say, Wherein have we polluted thee? In that ye say, The table of the LORD is contemptible."

PART TWO
NEW TESTAMENT

MATTHEW 6:7

"But when ye pray, use not vain repetitions, as the heathen do..."

MARK 6:7

"And he called unto him the twelve, and began to send them forth by two and two; and gave them power over unclean spirits..."

LUKE 6:7

"**A**nd the scribes and Pharisees watched him, whether he would heal on the sabbath day..."

JOHN 6:7

"**P**hilip answered him, *Two hundred pennyworth of bread is not sufficient for them…*"

ACTS 6:7

"And the word of God increased; and the number of the disciples multiplied in Jerusalem greatly…"

ROMANS 6:7

" F or he that is dead is freed from sin."

1 CORINTHIANS 6:7

" *N* ow therefore there is utterly a fault among you, because ye go to law one with another…"

2 CORINTHIANS 6:7

"By the word of truth, by the power of God, by the armour of righteousness…"

GALATIANS 6:7

"Be not deceived: God is not mocked: for whatsoever a man soweth, that shall he also reap."

EPHESIANS 6:7

"With good will doing service, as to the Lord, and not to men..."

PHILIPPIANS 1:6-7

"Being confident of this very thing, that he which hath begun a good work in you will perform it until the day of Jesus Christ: Even as it is meet for me to think this of you all, because I have you in my heart; inasmuch as both in my bonds, and in the defence and confirmation of the gospel, ye all are partakers of my grace."

COLOSSIANS 1:6–7

"Which is come unto you, as it is in all the world; and bringeth forth fruit, as it doth also in you, since the day ye heard of it, and knew the grace of God in truth: As ye also learned of Epaphras our dear fellowservant, who is for you a faithful minister of Christ..."

1 THESSALONIANS 1:6–7

"**A**nd ye became followers of us, and of the Lord, having received the word in much affliction, with joy of the Holy Ghost: So that ye were examples to all that believe in Macedonia and Achaia."

2 THESSALONIANS 1:6–7

"*S*eeing it is a righteous thing with God to recompense tribulation to them that trouble you; And to you who are troubled rest with us, when the Lord Jesus shall be revealed from heaven with his mighty angels...*"

1 TIMOTHY 6:7

"For we brought nothing into this world, and it is certain we can carry nothing out."

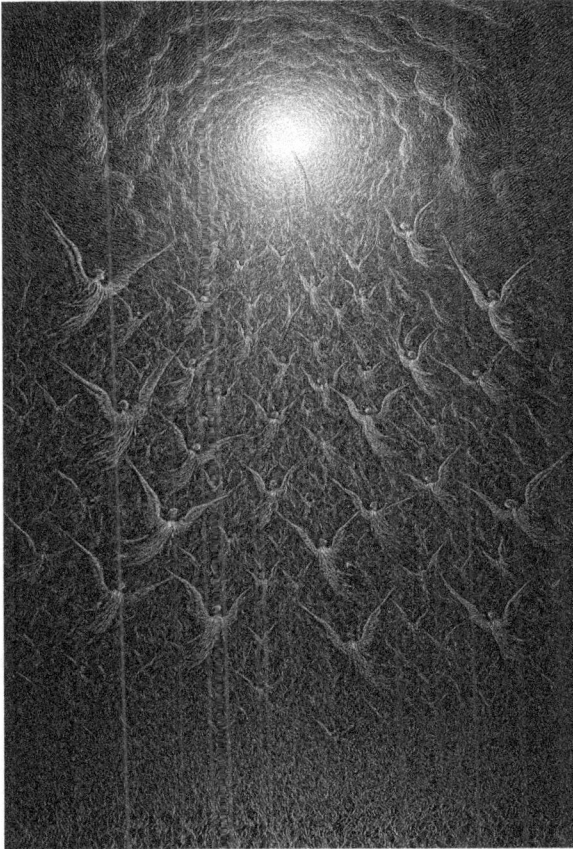

2 TIMOTHY 1:6–7

"Wherefore I put thee in remembrance that thou stir up the gift of God, which is in thee by the putting on of my hands. For God hath not given us the spirit of fear; but of power, and of love, and of a sound mind."

TITUS 1:6–7

"If any be blameless, the husband of one wife, having faithful children not accused of riot or unruly. For a bishop must be blameless, as the steward of God; not selfwilled, not soon angry, not given to wine, no striker, not given to filthy lucre..."

PHILEMON 1:6–7

"That the communication of thy faith may become effectual by the acknowledging of every good thing which is in you in Christ Jesus. For we have great joy and consolation in thy love, because the bowels of the saints are refreshed by thee, brother."

HEBREWS 6:7

"For the earth which drinketh in the rain that cometh oft upon it..."

JAMES 1:6–7

"**B**ut let him ask in faith, nothing wavering. For he that wavereth is like a wave of the sea driven with the wind and tossed. For let not that man think that he shall receive any thing of the Lord."

1 PETER 1:6–7

W herein ye greatly rejoice, though now for a season, if need be, ye are in heaviness through manifold temptations: That the trial of your faith, being much more precious than of gold that perisheth, though it be tried with fire, might be found unto praise and honour and glory at the appearing of Jesus Christ..."

2 PETER 1:6–7

"*And to knowledge temperance; and to temperance patience; and to patience godliness; and to godliness brotherly kindness; and to brotherly kindness charity.*"

1 JOHN 1:6–7

"I f we say that we have fellowship with him, and walk in darkness, we lie, and do not the truth: But if we walk in the light, as he is in the light, we have fellowship one with another, and the blood of Jesus Christ his Son cleanseth us from all sin."

2 JOHN 1:6–7

"And this is love, that we walk after his commandments. This is the commandment, That, as ye have heard from the beginning, ye should walk in it. For many deceivers are entered into the world, who confess not that Jesus Christ is come in the flesh. This is a deceiver and an antichrist."

3 JOHN 1:6–7

"Which have borne witness of thy charity before the church: whom if thou bring forward on their journey after a godly sort, thou shalt do well: because that for his name's sake they went forth, taking nothing of the Gentiles."

JUDE 1:6–7

"**A**nd the angels which kept not their first estate, but left their own habitation, he hath reserved in everlasting chains under darkness unto the judgment of the great day. Even as Sodom and Gomorrha, and the cities about them in like manner, giving themselves over to fornication, and going after strange flesh, are set forth for an example, suffering the vengeance of eternal fire."

REVELATION 6:7

"And when he had opened the fourth seal, I heard the voice of the fourth beast say, Come and see."